DISCOVERIES
IN
MARTIN'S
HUNDRED

COLONIAL WILLIAMSBURG ARCHAEOLOGICAL SERIES NO. 10

DISCOVERIES IN MARTIN'S HUNDRED

by
Ivor Noël Hume

The Colonial Williamsburg Foundation
Williamsburg, Virginia

Library of Congress Cataloging in Publication Data

Noël Hume, Ivor.
  Discoveries in Martin's Hundred.

  (Colonial Williamsburg archaeological series; no. 10)
  1. Martin's Hundred Site (Va.)   2. Carter's Grove (Va.)
  3. Wolstenholme Towne (Va.) I. Title. II. Series.
  F234.M378N6257   1983   975.5′425   83-1951
  ISBN 0-87935-069-5

Cover photograph: The Wolstenholme site as interpreted to Carter's Grove visitors.

PREFACE

Carter's Grove plantation was deeded to the Colonial Williamsburg Foundation in 1969. Beginning in June of the following year and continuing until March 1972, its department of archaeology mounted a field survey of the plantation's more than five hundred acres in search of lost structures and evidences of life on the property in the eighteenth century. The fruits of that survey were less plentiful than might have been expected, and when it came time to summarize them for publication in the Foundation's eighth in its series of archaeological booklets, the title had to reflect the search rather than its results: *Digging for Carter's Grove*.

The final paragraph of that booklet hinted at other archaeological stories still to be told, and at questions that could only be answered by further digging. "But because the questions are not germane to the plantation's eighteenth-century history," I wrote, "the search for the answers has been deferred. They are questions relating to prehistory and to the seventeenth century, when Carter's Grove land served as an Indian burial ground and as the scene of early colonial occupation in at least four scattered areas." That was a cautiously couched understatement, and any reader looking carefully at the map at the back of the booklet would have seen that the marked areas of seventeenth-century occupation were more extensive than the sum of those from the eighteenth century.

Time and again the survey team's trenches and test pits had turned up pottery and other artifacts dating from the first half of the seventeenth century. To most archaeologists, stumbling into a century earlier than one expects is cause for elation and the handing out of medals, yet at Carter's Grove I had no choice but to tell Dr. William M. Kelso, the crew supervisor, that finding more about the early sites was not part of our mission.

Four years would slip by before we returned to Carter's Grove, this time with the crew under the supervision of senior archaeologist Eric Klingelhofer. Once again the mission was not to seek out the seventeenth century; what was needed was an assurance that a hitherto unexcavated area northeast of the eighteenth-century mansion could be used to set up exhibits devoted to contemporary colonial life without damaging any underlying archaeological remains. In short, it was hoped that nothing would be found.

Rarely in archaeology do projects turn out as one expects or wishes. More often than not the high hopes with which a dig begins turn to weary disappointment before it ends. This one was different. A project that began with such modest, even negative, goals was destined to succeed beyond all hopes, yielding one spectacular discovery after another.

A preliminary account of what was being found was published in the *National Geographic Magazine* in June 1979, followed by another in January 1982. These, coupled with broad and sustained press interest, kept Carter's Grove in the public eye as the digging progressed. But like many another chance survival and lucky discovery, the sites of the seventeenth-century settlements in Martin's Hundred (later Carter's Grove) assumed a not entirely justified importance. Nevertheless, all concerned had much for which to be thankful—including the opportunity to follow a hesitant *Digging for Carter's Grove* with the more positive *Discoveries in Martin's Hundred*.

For the benefit of those who may wish to use the illustrated artifacts for comparative purposes or who need to cite them as parallels in their own publications, the catalog numbers and key measurements are listed on pages 63-64.

AN
ACKNOWLEDGMENT

The Martin's Hundred excavations would have ended in the fall of 1976 had not the National Geographic Society's chairman emeritus, Dr. Melville Bell Grosvenor, taken a personal interest in the project. His enthusiasm was soon to be translated into financial support from the Society that would continue through three more years of digging and into the all-important period of post-excavation research.

That Dr. Grosvenor did not live to see the work completed is cause for the deepest regret.

DISCOVERIES
IN
MARTIN'S
HUNDRED

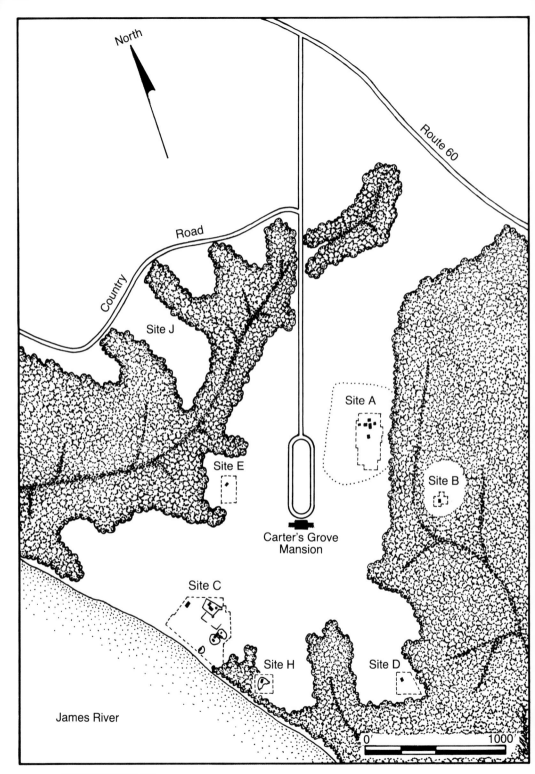

FRONTISPIECE.
The principal Martin's Hundred sites excavated or discovered between 1976 and 1981.

ON BOTH SIDES OF THIS ROAD AND
EXTENDING WEST WAS THE PLANTA-
TION KNOWN AS MARTIN'S HUNDRED,
ORIGINALLY OF 80,000 ACRES. SETTLED
IN 1619, THIS HUNDRED SENT DELE-
GATES TO THE FIRST LEGISLATIVE AS-
SEMBLY IN AMERICA, 1619. IN THE
INDIAN MASSACRE OF 1622, SEVENTY-
EIGHT WERE SLAIN HERE.

Embossed on a state marker few visitors stopped to read, this information was, for decades, all that most Virginians knew, or wanted to know, about Martin's Hundred. That two in five of its "facts" proved to be wrong is a measure of how much Colonial Williamsburg archaeologists had to learn about a place whose cumbersome name and tangled story they were to bring belatedly to the attention of American historians.

One has only to attempt to recall everything one did last year to realize that recorded history is patched together from well-remembered highlights and the chance survival of bits and pieces of doubtful importance. The story of Martin's Hundred survived not on library shelves but buried in and stained into the ground—where by chance and not by design archaeologists

FIGURE 1.

Typical post-hole patterns for buildings and fences as revealed on the site of the "Company Compound" at Site C.

would find it *(Figure 1)*. That accident of discovery, more than its political or economic importance to the Virginia colony, has earned Martin's Hundred a seat at the table of history.

Had the later court records for James City County not been destroyed, and had archaeologists digging at Jamestown found the site and remains of its early palisaded settlement, Martin's Hundred would have remained just another private plantation established by British entrepreneurs in the second decade of the colony's existence. In the absence, however, of all but the merest trace of the first Jamestown settlements, and lacking the wills and inventories that are the historian's principal window on the way Virginians lived in early colonial times, the discovery of the defenses, homes, domestic garbage, and the dead of Martin's Hundred assume unexpected significance.

Although many American children (and most British children, too, for that matter) assume that the history of the United States began in 1620 with the arrival at Plymouth, Massachusetts, of the *Mayflower* and its supposed shipload of freedom-seeking pilgrims, the story really began in London fourteen years earlier. In 1606 King James I granted a charter to a group of British businessmen known as merchant adventurers, giving them the exclusive right to seize and settle wherever they fancied across the American continent between the 34th and 45th parallels. Incorporated as the Virginia Company of London, they sent out their first three ships in the fall of that year, promising themselves a handsome return on their investment ten years later.

When in 1616 dividend time came around, there was no money to distribute; instead, the Company's officials had to tell the stockholders that if the Virginia enterprise was to survive, more money was needed, and needed quickly. Although very little had gone right for the Company in its first ten years, it had one undeniable asset—land. In the eyes of the English (Indian rights notwithstanding), they owned the American continent westward from tidewater Virginia to the "Sea of China and the Indies." According to a 1651 map—the only one showing Martin's Hundred—that western sea could be reached "in ten dayes march . . . from the head of Ieames River" *(Figure 2)*. The Virginia Company obtained royal permission to set up subsidiary companies to be formed by single individuals or corporations like itself, the size of their holdings to be determined by the number of shares that each purchased. Priced at twelve pounds ten shillings, one share secured one hundred acres of Virginia land.

The group who incorporated themselves into the Society of Martin's Hundred was large enough to be assigned twenty thousand acres, and late in 1618 they boarded 220 settlers onto the ship *Gift of God* and sent it forth, confident, one supposes, that these people would succeed where so many before them had failed. By comparison with the 104 colonists whom the Virginia Company had relied on to secure an American foothold in 1606, the Martin's Hundred enterprise was a formidable and finely focused investment in both faith and fortune.

The Society seems to have been named for Richard Martin, recorder of the City of London, who died before the *Gift of God* reached land. If that was a portent of disasters soon to come,

FIGURE 2.
Detail adapted from the Farrer map of Virginia. Although published in 1651, it still showed the location of Martin's Hundred (circled) which, by then, had long since ceased to be a private company venture.

Martin's death mattered little to the Society. He had served his purpose. His name on its prospectus had helped bring together the largest number of investors in any of the secondary companies. More important was another name, that of Sir John Wolstenholme, a respected and vigorous figure in most of Britain's expansionist efforts in the early years of the seventeenth century. He was a member of the East India Company, a backer of Henry Hudson's ill-fated 1610 voyage in search of a Northwest Passage and of William Baffin's expedition five years later. Both voyages had earned him a place in cartographic history, Hudson naming a cape for him, and Baffin a Greenland sound and a nearby island. Sir John's interest in the Bermuda branch of the Virginia Company won him a small bay where his name survived, albeit in an increasingly distorted form, until the mid-eighteenth century. It was only to be expected, therefore, that as a leading shareholder in the Society of Martin's Hundred, he should get his name on the map of Virginia. Grateful friends saw to it that he did; they named the Society's administrative center Wolstenholme Towne (*Figure 3*).

FIGURE 3.
Sir John Wolstenholme's contributions to North American exploration and colonization earned him several place names from Greenland to Bermuda.

Getting there—anywhere—in the seventeenth century could be a hazardous undertaking, and although the harshness of life in those days made people far more willing to take chances than we are today, a voyage to America was recognizably risky. Consequently, the number of settlers coaxed aboard in England might have differed markedly from the tally of those who arrived alive in Virginia. Indeed, it is thought likely that the number of Martin's Hundred colonists who stepped ashore at Jamestown in 1619 was far smaller than the 220 who left England. If that can be proved to be so, there is reason to deduce that they did not begin construction of Wolstenholme Towne until their "Governor," William Harwood, arrived in August 1620. Without a Society-appointed leader to present its credentials to the Virginia Company's governor at Jamestown, the latter may well have delayed issuing the twenty thousand acres of land that had been promised to the Society's shareholders—in which case 1619 slipped away without anything being accomplished.

It was a Virginia Company rule that although no restriction was placed on the number of shares sold or on the number of hundred-acre parcels into which its officers carved up the homeland of Virginia's Indians, no plantation was to be located within ten miles of any other. The Martin's Hundred holdings included (according to a repatenting document of 1622) ten miles of frontage along the James River with Wolstenholme Towne in the middle of it—five miles from its nearest neighbor downstream toward Newport News, and five miles up toward the settlement at Archer's Hope, and snuggling in the curve of the river below Jamestown Island. It was then, as it has ever since remained, a very desirable piece of real estate, a fine waterfront property backed by flat, arable land fed by an abundance of freshwater springs. Wolstenholme Towne, like its eighteenth-century successor, the mansion of Carter's Grove, was strategically placed to spot unfriendly ships sailing up the river long before they came in cannon range (*Figure 4*). In short, the Martin's Hundred lands could not be bettered. All they needed to turn a handsome profit for their London owners were hardworking and well-led settlers, good weather, good relations with the "salvages," and an absence of Spaniards.

FIGURE 4.
A 1970 aerial view of Carter's Grove plantation and (lettered) the locations of Sites A, B, C, and H.

17

18

The Spaniards stayed away, but relations with the Indians deteriorated, as did the health of the settlers. Although the Society claimed to have sent out 280 colonists, by the winter of 1621–1622 their number was put at 140, and by the evening of March 22 they could muster fewer than seventy. That morning, pushed beyond endurance, the Indians of the Tidewater led by Chief Opechancanough rose against the English, killing them in the fields and in their homes all the way from the falls at modern Richmond to the ocean at Newport News. The colony's leaders at Jamestown had been warned several hours before the attacks began, but not, it seems, in time to pass the warning on to all their neighbors along the river. Martin's Hundred, only nine miles downstream, was among the hardest hit—as Colonial Williamsburg archaeologists would frequently be reminded when they uncovered the burned remains of buildings and the bones of the dead.

The excavations began in 1976 and continued into the first days of 1981. By then six sites had been fully explored. All of them dated between about 1620 and 1645. It would have been convenient if they had been investigated in sequence, but unfor-

FIGURE 5. *Post-hole patterns for the principal buildings at Site A.*

tunately one only learns the age of a site by digging it. In Martin's Hundred, fate in the shape of Colonial Williamsburg's interpretive needs caused the archaeologists to begin at the site that proved to have been most recently inhabited, and, being the first to be explored, they had no choice but to name it Site A (*see Frontispiece*).

Late and early are, of course, relative terms. To most American historical archaeologists, Site A was very early indeed. It had been abandoned by about 1645. Site B, across a ravine to the east, was only slightly earlier in date but very different in character. Its inhabitants were gone by about 1640. Site E was hard to date, but its lifespan probably kept it in the 1625–1635 bracket. The rest were earlier still, colonial occupation at Sites C, D, and H having opened and closed in the two or three years that ended with the Indian uprising of 1622.

Had the archaeologists been able to excavate the Martin's Hundred sites in chronological order, evolutionary trends in building construction and artifact design would have been more easily detected. On the credit side, however, Site A proved to be an excellent training ground for a team whose previous experience had been largely confined to unearthing the easily interpreted brick foundations of eighteenth-century buildings in Williamsburg. The legacy of Martin's Hundred was very different. No matter whether the excavators were finding the remains of something once as substantial as a fort or as slender as a corn crib, they survived as mere shadows in the clay, ghost images that vanished as the sun came up to dry the earth.

Unlike the buildings of Williamsburg, most of which were erected on continuous brick foundations, the homes and indeed all the early structures in Martin's Hundred had been erected around posts seated in the earth (*Figure 5*). When the houses burned or fell down, their posts rotted away to leave molds in the ground that filled with loam, and in the yellow clay of tidewater Virginia they remained as darker stains against the light. Only by carefully scraping and wetting the sun-baked clay could these traces be found—a backbreaking and morale-bending task that went on for months at a time with little to show for it but a few more post-hole dots on the map. Slowly, however, patterns began to emerge.

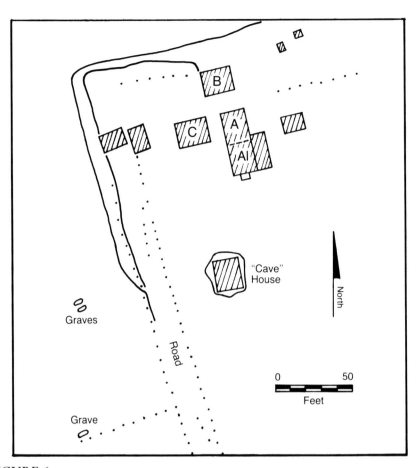

FIGURE 6.

A simplified plan of Site A showing the principal dwelling (A) and its extension (A1), its primary companion buildings (B and C), the post-flanked approach road, and adjacent graves.

At Site A three groups of six large holes became a trio of buildings of identical size: twenty feet by eighteen. Later one of them was doubled in length, and at forty feet by eighteen it became a relatively large house—at least by early seventeenth-century Virginia standards *(Figure 6)*. By comparison with the size of the only house in Martin's Hundred whose measurements are recorded in surviving documents, a home built for servant Richard Chelsey that measured only twelve feet by ten, the big house at Site A was a mansion. From garbage pits adjacent to it came artifacts attesting to the quality of the place: an imported ceramic fireplace tile, part of a pair of decorative tongs with

20

which to feed the fire *(Figure 7)*, broken panes from glass windows, and, more importantly as it turned out, strips of the lead that had held them in position.

The lead's significance took four years to be appreciated. Unlike excavated iron that deteriorates rapidly if it does not receive prompt laboratory treatment, lead (if it survives at all) does not cry out for immediate conservation. Consequently, the window lead was among the last of Site A's artifacts to receive the conservator's attention. When he eventually began to straighten the bent strips and to clean out the dirt trapped in their folds, he revealed a long and frequently repeated inscription hidden inside. It read "Iohn: Byshopp of Exceter Gonner : 1625 :" *(Figure 8)*.

FIGURE 7.
Part of a pair of fireplace tongs enriched with a brass collar and stamped decoration. From Site A; about 1640.

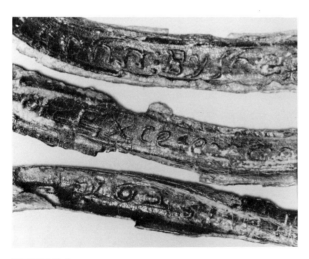

FIGURE 8.
Enlarged details of inscriptions embossed within the folds of window lead from Site A. Dated 1625, this is the earliest recorded example of a practice whose purpose has yet to be explained.

21

The identity of John Byshopp and the meaning of the word Gonner have yet to be established, but there is nothing equivocal about the date, proving as it does that windows in the house at Site A were installed or replaced no earlier than 1625. If, as seems likely, John Byshopp was a maker of glaziers' vises, it is probable that the owner (if not the builder) of the Site A house had imported prefabricated windows from Exeter in Devonshire.

John Byshopp's window lead was not the only Devonshire import to reach Martin's Hundred. Its governor, William Harwood, came from Barnstaple on Devon's north coast. Two more clues hint that it was he who built the house on Site A—a cannonball and a tag from a garter.

A 1625 inventory of Virginia's military assets listed only one cannon in Martin's Hundred, and that was in the custody of William Harwood. The census entry described it as a "Peece of Ordnance, I wth all things thereto belonging" and clearly the "things" had to include projectiles such as the six and three-quarter-pound ball from Site A *(Figure 9)*. The garter tag's evidence was less direct. Woven from threads of gold, the tag was one of many that dangled from each garter of any well-dressed male in the early seventeenth century *(Figure 10)*. But only some men were allowed to be richly dressed in Virginia, for

FIGURE 9.

An iron cannonball of a size to fit a gun of saker caliber. Found at Site A, the ball may have been ammunition for the "Peece of Ordnance" listed in William Harwood's 1625 inventory.

FIGURE 10.

Threads of silver and a garter "point" of woven gold (below), the latter from clothing and garters of the quality depicted by Daniel Mytens in his 1621 portrait of Sir Henry Paiton (arrowed). From Site A; about 1625–1645.

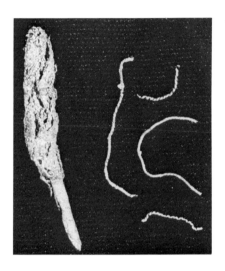

in 1621 the governor received instructions from London that "no person residing in Virginia (excepting those of y^e Counsill And heads of Hundreds and plantations ther wyues & Chilldren) shall weare any gold in ther Clothes." Harwood was then both a council member and the head of his hundred.

None of this was proof positive. The cannonball could have been stolen from Harwood and used to grind corn, and his golden garter may have ended its life on a scarecrow in somebody else's field. But an archaeologist has to reconstruct the past from a multitude of such fragments, and if he rejects all whose evidence is not irrefutable, rarely will he be able to draw a conclusion about anything. Instead, he must do the best he can with what he finds, careful always to lard his language with qualifiers: perhapses, possiblies, and it-is-likely-thats. In Martin's Hundred, where the documentary evidence is as fragmentary as its pottery, the search for truth will continue for many years, and from time to time early thoughts will be questioned and preliminary conclusions reassessed.

Social historians may discover why, for example, fragments of more than a hundred glass bottles were found at Site A *(Figure 11)* when no early Virginia domestic inventory lists more than six. They will learn more about early trade and the significance of Iberian earthenware bottles found on the same site *(Figure 12)*, and why anyone thought it necessary to import Dutch kitchenwares *(Figures 13 and 14)* when local Virginia potters had no trouble making pots that did the job just as well.

FIGURE 11.

(Below) Square-bodied glass bottles like this were plentiful at Site A and would have been used as containers for liquids of all kinds.

FIGURE 12.

A poorly fired earthenware bottle from Site A, decorated on each side with a crudely painted blue star under a lead glaze. Probably Spanish; about 1625–1645.

FIGURE 13.

(Right) Detail from The Poultry Yard *(1660) by Dutch artist Jan Steen, showing a green and yellow glazed "milk pot" almost identical to the antique example illustrated in Figure 14 (right).*

FIGURE 14.

(Above) A Dutch "milk pot" from Site A of the same type as, but slightly more medieval in style than, the example shown in Jan Steen's painting (top, right), or the intact antique (right), and therefore thought to be older. About 1625–1645.

25

FIGURE 15.
An earthenware alembic, the top element from a distilling apparatus. Lead-glazed on the inside and skillfully shaped by a local potter, this rare object is one of the earliest and most sophisticated examples of colonial potting yet found in America. From Site A; about 1625–1645.

The discovery that lead-glazed earthenwares as sophisticated as those used in England were being made in Martin's Hundred before 1622 was to be one of the archaeologists' most important revelations. An almost intact alembic used in distilling is the most spectacular example of early American potting yet found *(Figure 15)*. It came from a pit on Site A, which also contained waste from a potter's workshop, and thus prompted a search for the kiln in which it was baked, a search that led across a ravine to the east into a heavily wooded area to be named Site B.

Unlike the open field of Site A, Site B had escaped the plow and had remained undisturbed since it was abandoned around 1640 and the trees grew over it. With the ground laced with roots and protected by standing timber, digging was slow but the rewards were spectacular. Artifacts of fine quality were scattered all through the soil layers that had accumulated during the site's seventeenth-century occupation. A fingernail-sized frag-

FIGURE 16.
A large gray stoneware jug imported from the Westerwald district of the Rhineland. Decorated with cobalt, the type is paralleled in several Dutch paintings of the mid-seventeenth century. From Site B; discarded about 1631.

FIGURE 17.

Part of a locally made slipware dish; one of three represented by fragments from Site B. With the year 1631 worked into the yellow design, this is the oldest dated example of American pottery yet recorded.

ment of a German stoneware jug was found within the only building discovered there. The rest of the jug (save for a few missing fragments) was discovered in a nearby rubbish pit *(Figure 16)*, suggesting that the vessel had been broken in the house and the pieces swept up and tossed into a hole in the yard.

Finding the post-hole pattern defining the Site B house was a major accomplishment, but it did little to mitigate the gloom that hung like a gray cloud over the archaeologists as the digging went on and the hoped-for pottery kiln declined to be found. Some consolation came from the same pit that had yielded the fine German jug. Lying at the bottom were pieces from a locally made slipware dish marked 1631—the earliest dated example of American pottery yet found, and among the small handful of surviving English slipwares bearing dates prior to 1640 *(Figure 17)*.

28

FIGURE 18.
(Left) A detail from Sir Anthony van Dyck's 1641 portrait of Charles II, aged eleven. The elbow elements of his armor are similar to one found at Site B (below) in a context of about 1631.

FIGURE 19.
An armored vest comprising several hundred small iron plates riveted to fabric and overlapping like tiles on a roof. Many such plates were found on Martin's Hundred sites. Called a brigandine, the illustrated garment is thought to be Italian and to date from the sixteenth century.

29

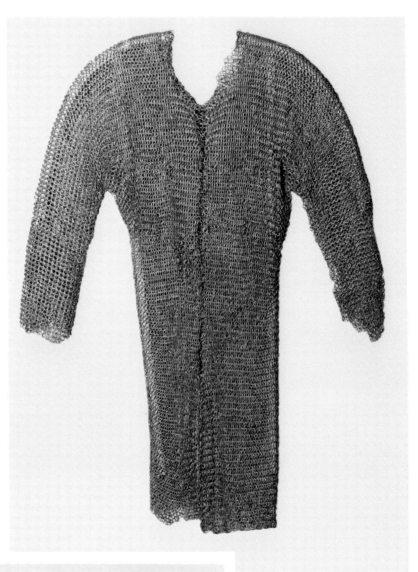

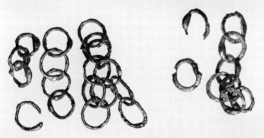

FIGURE 20.

A typical shirt of mail and (left) examples of similarly riveted mail links from Site B; deposited around 1631.

Just as artifacts from Site A had hinted at the presence there of someone of importance, so Site B sent a similar message. Part of a gilded spur, table knives encrusted with silver and inlaid with gold, and an elbow section from a suit of armor more elaborate than was possessed by most Virginia colonists—all spoke of wealth *(Figure 18)*. At first thought to be a relic of the 1622 Indian attack, the iron elbow came from the same pit as the 1631 dish and so could not have been discarded before that date. With the couter (as armor's elbow elements are called) were small iron plates once riveted into a canvas jacket known as a brigandine *(Figure 19)*; so, too, were several well-preserved links of mail. Such plates and links would be found on most of Martin's Hundred sites, and the documentary evidence of the 1625 census shows that several households in the hundred were equipped with "Coats of Steele" or "Coats of Male" *(Figure 20)*. By far the most significant pieces of armor, however, came from the site that the archaeologists believed to be that of the community's administrative and military center at Wolstenholme Towne *(Figure 21)*.

FIGURE 21.

(Overleaf) Artist Richard Schlecht's reconstruction showing that part of Site C tentatively identified as Wolstenholme Towne as it may have looked around 1621. The scene shows the fort from the wooded high ground behind the settlement, to the right of it the "Company Barn," to the left the "Company Compound" with its longhouse and store building, and beyond that a house that the archaeologists named "The Domestic Unit." The painting interprets only what was found and shows the James River shoreline where it is today. In reality, as many as half of the Wolstenholme buildings may have been lost to erosion.

There, in the silt of a shallow well within the palisaded fort, lay the first face-covering helmet to be found in the New World *(Figure 22)*. Although time and moisture had reduced the metal to flaking rust, techniques developed specifically for the job enabled the helmet to be lifted safely from the ground and carried to Colonial Williamsburg's archaeological laboratory to be preserved *(Figure 23)*. Finding the helmet cast new light on the military attitudes of emigrant Englishmen in the early seventeenth century, and subsequent research added credence to the notion that settlers sent from England were supplied with both equipment and instructions based on previous, but not always relevant, European experience—hence the helmet that would have baked the head of its wearer on any summer day in Virginia.

It is true that both Sir Walter Raleigh and John Smith circulated lists of the kinds of kits and craftsmen needed for successful settling in America, and it is equally true that plantation planners made use of them. There persisted, nevertheless, a deep-seated conviction that although native Americans might be a nuisance, Spaniards were the real threat. If the English settlers were deployed, equipped, and drilled to defeat comparably armed and trained Spanish invaders, it followed as surely as big fish eat little fish that Virginia's Indians posed no problem.

Ever since the world's first invading army burned the first noncombatant's house, civilian populations have demanded protection for homes, livestock, and wives. Solutions developed in remote antiquity were still valid in the seventeenth century A.D. One either built a defense work around the entire settlement or constructed a fortress into which the population could flee in time of trouble. The former was the genesis of the medieval walled city; the latter the baron's castle with his tenants' cottages clustered outside its walls like chickens around a hen. Castles were cheaper if somewhat elitist, insuring that their owners' homes were defended but leaving the lesser folks to save only their necks. From the safety of the battlements they could see their houses burn and their possessions looted. In Virginia, Jamestown was the walled city while Wolstenholme Towne and other like settlements paralleled the castle-and-

FIGURE 22.

Called a close helmet because it closed over the wearer's face, this was the first of its kind to be found intact in the New World. Discarded around 1622.

FIGURE 23.

Preparing the fort's helmet to be lifted, still bedded in silt, and carried to the laboratory. Encased in a steel frame, the fragile remains were first shielded with a rubber compound and then reinforced with plaster of paris.

36

village concept. Thus when the Indians attacked in 1622, the previously warned Jamestown survived and so, it seems, did the fort at Wolstenholme—but the buildings outside it did not.

The archaeologists concluded that as much as half the Wolstenholme Towne settlement has been lost to river erosion, but unless that is a very conservative estimate, the "towne" was never more than a village with a population of about forty people. All its walls were of wood, and so, too, were its chimneys, the houses being timber framed and the spaces between filled with wattles and clay. Roofs, of which no traces survived, were probably of thatch, bark, or perhaps wood shingles.

Only one small building *(Figure 21, left foreground)* suggests the typical home of a Martin's Hundred employee. The other buildings whose sites survive are thought to have been associated with company business: a store, a barn or produce warehouse, and perhaps a communal dwelling having a stable at one end *(Figure 21, right foreground)*. All these structures are

FIGURE 24.

The site of the small dwelling called the "Domestic Unit." To the left of it stretches an oval line of post-holes thought to mark the location of a light wattle fence surrounding a shade tree.

FIGURE 25.

Post-hole lines representing part of the fort's east and south walls as revealed in 1977. To the top left are holes for the supposed watchtower, and in front of them a rectangular rubbish pit, the well, and the later cattle pond. To the right are several holes subsequently found to have been part of the fort's only large building.

represented only by the earth-filled holes in which their posts had been seated *(Figure 24)*; consequently, their on-paper reconstruction owes more to educated guesswork and paralleling information from other sources than it does to irrefutable archaeological proof.

The fort was trapezoidal with a watchtower at one corner, a gun platform at another, and perhaps a projecting flanker at a third. All this could be read from the post-holes, as could the location of gates where the posts were set closer together than the standard nine-foot placement along the lines of the uninterrupted walls *(Figure 25)*. In 1610 William Strachey described the palisades at Jamestown as being constructed from "Plankes and strong Posts, foure foote deep in the ground, of Yong Oakes, Walnuts, &c." He noted, too, that "at every Angle or corner, where the lines meete, a Bulwarke or Watchtower" was built. Although the Wolstenholme Towne fort was much smaller, covering only about 10,050 square feet as against early Jamestown's sometimes estimated 42,800 square feet, Strachey's description of a palisade built from posts set in the ground (presumably with rails spanning between them to which palings were attached) offered a perfect interpretation of the post-hole evidence at the Wolstenholme fort, as did his description of watchtowers and flankers that provided protection against attackers assaulting the walls *(Figure 26)*.

The gun platform was less easy to interpret, yet its position was ideally situated to fire between the buildings of the "Company Compound" and the isolated domestic unit. By standing on a stepladder at the gun's estimated height above the ground, one could clearly see that it had a commanding view down the river. But the river was farther away in the seventeenth century than it is today and it would have taken a big gun to fire with any accuracy at approaching enemy ships. That Martin's Hundred had possessed a large cannon had been suggested by the discovery of the cannonball on Site A *(Figure 9)*, by a gun having an eight- to nine-foot barrel—and that was the problem. When discharged, large cannon were likely to recoil half the length of their barrels, enough for the Wolstenholme gun to fall off the back of the platform! The solution to that enigma lay, not in the fort, but in the next field downriver on a site that was still to be found.

The character of the dwelling inside the fort remains equally enigmatic; indeed, its post-holes add up to the least convincing building found on any of the Martin's Hundred sites. On the other hand, the artifacts found in the nearby cattle pond and well point to the presence of someone important, such as William Harwood, the settlement's leader.

Most significant among the fort's artifacts were several fragments from a cast-iron fireback decorated with the arms of James I *(Figure 27)*. Such an object would only have been brought over by someone having social aspirations. Almost as

FIGURE 26.

The fort viewed from the southeast corner at the completion of excavation in 1978.

FIGURE 27.

A modern reproduction of a 1621 cast-iron fireback decorated with the arms of James I. Several fragments from an almost identical fireback were found in and around the fort.

FIGURE 28.

The neck and base from apparently identical jugs of Rhenish blue and gray stoneware, the neck from the fort well and the base from Site A. The handle is stamped WM, presumably the potter's initials. The neck was discarded around 1622.

FIGURE 29.
The site of the "Company Barn" as seen from the northeast.

instructive was the neck and handle from a blue and gray stoneware jug from the German Rhineland *(Figure 28)*. The base from an apparently identical jug had previously been found at Site A, the supposed Harwood plantation site. That two disassociated settlers would have brought over jugs made by the same German potter was too great a coincidence to be taken seriously. Much easier to accept was the notion that the fort and Site A had been occupied by the same person who broke one jug on one site and its twin on the other.

The largest of Wolstenholme Towne's surviving building sites proved not to lie within the safety of the fort but outside it to the northwest. With its roof supported on three large posts and reaching to the ground, this structure is believed to have been the Company barn where produce could be stored before being carried down to the river and shipped to Jamestown and home to England *(Figure 29)*.

Only the barn's forty-five feet by twenty-nine feet, six inch dimensions and the character of its construction helped identify it as such. No artifacts were found inside it. That was in marked contrast to the "Company Compound" where a large pit yielded many of the most important objects yet recovered from an early English colonial site *(Figure 30)*.

It is not always the largest and most photogenic artifacts that have the most to say. From the "Company Compound" pit came five small lead seals once attached to fabric imported from Augsburg in Germany *(Figure 31)*. That so many were identically marked suggested that the seals came from Company supplies rather than from the household of a single settler. It was this deduction that first led the excavators to dub the impaled area the "Company Compound."

FIGURE 30.
A miscellany of iron and ceramic artifacts lay crowded together in the "Potter's Pond."

FIGURE 31.

Lead seals found in the "Potter's Pond" bear the initial and emblem of the German city of Augsburg and probably came from bales of fabric called fustian. Discarded around 1620–1622.

A potter had worked within the compound and evidence is strong that it was he who dug the pit, probably to obtain clay. With the first rain it filled with water and before long the resulting pond became a convenient place for dumping trash, much of it the potter's own—including an iron tool that was at first hard to identify *(Figure 32)*. Fragments of the kiln structure were found, as were large numbers of broken pots, some fired too hard and others not hard enough. All were valuable evidence of the capabilities of the earliest British colonial potter whose workplace has been found *(Figure 33)*. The iron tool turned out to be a blunger, an instrument used by potters to cut and stir their clay as they mixed it in water-filled pits. It is the oldest of its kind yet known, a distinction it possesses only because it had the questionable luck to have been lost or thrown away before the Indians destroyed the settlement in 1622.

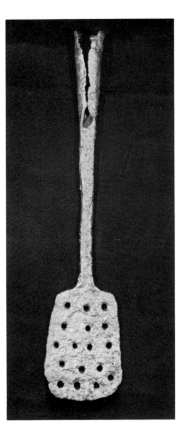

FIGURE 32.

This perforated iron tool once had a long wooden handle and was called a blunger. Found in the "Potter's Pond," it was used to mix clay and is one of the oldest surviving instruments of the English potters' craft. Discarded before March 22, 1622.

FIGURE 33.

Examples of the Martin's Hundred potter's art, all from the pond inside the "Company Compound." Discarded before March 22, 1622.

45

FIGURE 34.

An iron frying pan from the "Potter's Pond." Another of the same type with its thirty-inch handle intact was found in excavations at Mathews Manor several miles farther down the James River. Discarded around 1622.

FIGURE 35.

A skillet of copper-alloyed sheet metal found in the "Potter's Pond." Two iron legs and a third welded to an iron handle, all once riveted to the bowl, had been detached before it was discarded around 1622.

FIGURE 36.

The presence in the "Potter's Pond" of this undamaged iron bill was hard to explain. Such tools were used to lop trees. Deposited no later than 1622.

Although the pit came to be known as the "Potter's Pond," its treasures were not solely ceramic. Many were domestic: a decorated delftware ointment jar, an iron frying pan, a sheet-metal skillet without its iron legs and handle *(Figures 34 and 35)*, and the legs and handle from another that had lost its bowl. There was a bill of the kind used to prune fruit trees, the blade so well preserved that it was hard to imagine why anyone would have thrown it away *(Figure 36)*. Even more enigmatic was a broken barrel from a matchlock musket, but of such prodigious weight that the excavators first thought it was solid. X-ray photographs later revealed that it was packed from breech to the end of its broken barrel with small lead shot *(Figure 37)*.

The X-rays explained the barrel's weight, but in doing so they substituted another mystery: Why was the barrel packed with shot? The most obvious explanation had its documentation in the annals of the American Civil War, when, in the heat of battle, young and frightened soldiers with eyes shut sometimes thought that their guns had discharged when they had not. They then reloaded on the top of the first charge, only to have the gun again misfire. Records exist of guns being found packed with several charges, and Civil War enthusiasts who had heard about the "Potter's Pond" musket wrote offering that explanation. It was not the right one, however. This gun had not misfired as terrified settlers made their last stand against the Indians. It lacked both its breechblock and its priming pan. The X-rays showed no space for powder between the close-packed shot, but they did

FIGURE 37.

The breech end of a matchlock musket barrel and examples of the small lead shot found packed inside it. Discarded into the "Potter's Pond" no later than 1622.

show that the barrel had been heated sufficiently for the lead touching its walls to melt and fuse into a thin skin. Had gunpowder been so heated, it would have blown the lead out or have burst the barrel.

A more likely explanation seemed to be that the potter used fine lead shot in making his glaze. Supporting evidence was later forthcoming when a locally made mug was found to have a thick accumulation of glaze inside it, and, trapped within it, three pieces of lead shot of the same gauge as that removed from the gun barrel. There still remained the problem of why the potter would have stored his lead in so unmanageable a container. The answer may be that he was not storing it but temporarily using it to add weight to the gun barrel, which served him as a pestle to grind up frit used in making his glaze.

Even though the lead-filled gun barrel belied its military appearance, other artifacts from the pond did not. The scale-like plates from a brigandine were strewn down one side of the pit, apparently washed loose from their canvas jacket as the fabric slowly rotted in the mud. Fragments from an armor backplate lay close together, but in such positions, and with so many parts missing, that it must have been broken into pieces before being thrown away. Undamaged save for crushing due to ground pressure, and lying immediately below the fragmentary backplate, was an object which, when its side began to be uncovered, most resembled an iron cooking pot. It was too much to expect that Martin's Hundred might be about to surrender the New World's second close helmet. But it did.

The helmet lay on its side with its visor down and the handle of one of the potter's over-baked pipkins trapped under it. Thus the loss of the helmet and the potter's presence in the "Company Compound" were closely related. It was highly unlikely, however, that the helmet had belonged to the potter or even that the potter was a permanent resident of the compound. The armor was made for an officer and pointed to the presence there of someone in authority, whereas the quantity of spoiled pots was small enough to give credence to the theory that the potter was a temporary visitor who traveled from plantation to plantation, set up his kiln, made a batch of pots, and moved on.

48

Recovering the helmet from the fort well had taken the best part of two weeks, but by the time the second was found, the archaeologists had so improved their helmet-extracting technique that the job took less than four hours. There were no shortcuts once it reached the laboratory, however, and it took many weeks of careful conservation to reinforce the rust and to reshape the flattened visor *(Figure 38)*.

Even in its crushed condition, the helmet was clearly a helmet. Many of the other military artifacts from the "Potter's Pond" and elsewhere on the Martin's Hundred sites did not "read" nearly so easily. Because the end product of any archaeological excavation is the sharing of its information with a public not trained to "see" a whole object when shown only a dime-sized fragment, archaeologists and curators may have to go to

FIGURE 38.

The second close helmet after laboratory treatment. Discovered in the "Potter's Pond," it differs from the example found in the fort by having a less pronounced crest and lacking a prop to support the raised visor. Although the type is paralleled by helmets made in Austria in 1601, there is no reason to doubt that this specimen was made in England.

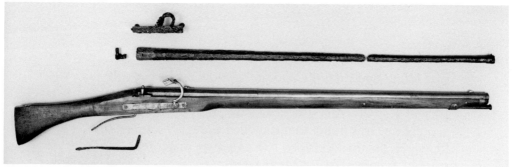

FIGURE 39.

Although no musket had been thrown away intact, all the necessary metal parts were represented among the artifacts from Site C: pan, lock, barrel, and trigger lever.

FIGURE 40.

Sword pommels and sword guards like the example from Site B (right) closely matched those of the antique broadsword (left) purchased to show how the parts fitted together. Early seventeenth century.

great lengths to bridge the gap. In books one can get away with drawings that sketch in the missing parts, but in a museum exhibit a musket trigger needs to share a case with a real gun of the same type *(Figure 39)*. Similarly, a sword guard that by itself looks like a bunch of rusted wires becomes eloquent only when laid beside an original weapon having an identical hilt *(Figure 40)*.

Through the generosity of friends, Colonial Williamsburg has been able to acquire several antique weapons to match the excavated fragments. In every instance save one, the artifact

49

was found and then the antique was donated or purchased. The exception was a powder flask from the collection of the late Harold L. Peterson, whose widow allowed the Foundation to acquire several items that included a dagger similar to a blade found in the fort *(Figure 41)* and two matchlock muskets to parallel fragments excavated from several sites. The Peterson Collection also contained a powder flask of the right period and type to augment any exhibit built around the muskets. Although the archaeologists had no matching fragment, Mrs. Peterson agreed to let the flask come to Williamsburg. Several weeks later the "Potter's Pond" yielded a badly decayed iron object which, when cleaned, proved to be the nozzle from just such a flask *(Figure 42)*.

Neither the military nor the domestic artifacts from the pond could reveal precisely when or under what circumstances they were abandoned. The clue to that was to be found in another hole in the ground, one located between the pond and the southeast door of the longhouse. The hole's narrow rectangular shape suggested that it might be a grave although domestic refuse in the top of it led some to identify it as a mere trash pit.

Ashes in post-holes of the longhouse indicated that the building had burned, and if the adjacent pit turned out to be a grave, it would be tempting to associate both burning and burying with the Indian assault on Martin's Hundred—tempting but dangerous. Accidental house fires were common among Virginia's early candlelit and combustible homes, and relatively few settlers died at the hands of the Indians. Indeed, a carefully dug grave might point more to a time when social niceties could be observed than to the chaotic aftermath of a massacre.

Standing beside the still earth-filled hole, the archaeologists defined the criteria needed to link the grave (if grave it was) to the longhouse fire, and to blame both on the Indians. First they needed a skeleton to prove the pit a grave. Then they needed to find artifacts in its filling that dated no later than 1622. Next they wanted convincing evidence that the occupant had not died of natural causes. Finally, they needed ashes under the skeleton, the ashes from the nearby ruin that almost certainly would have

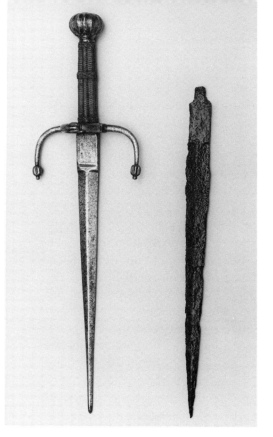

FIGURE 41.

The art of fencing as taught in the early seventeenth century called for two weapons, a sword in one hand and in the other a dagger. The latter, known as a main-gauche or left-hand dagger, was represented in the fort at Site C by a blade broken from its hilt. The type is closely paralleled by the sixteenth-century example (left).

FIGURE 42.

Early seventeenth-century muskets were loaded either with gunpowder measured into separate canisters or from flasks like the example (left) whose spouts were fitted with gates to isolate the quantity needed for each charge. The detached spout (right) was lost into the "Potter's Pond" before the Indian attack of 1622.

blown into the open hole as it waited to receive the corpse. All four needs were met *(Figure 43)*.

Broken tobacco pipes in the fill dated to the first decades of the seventeeth century, the skull of a male skeleton had been split by a blow between the eyes, and on the grave floor under his left leg lay small pieces of charcoal. There could be little doubt that the "Company Compound" had been destroyed in the uprising, or that the man in the grave was one of the more than fifty Martin's Hundred settlers who died on what a contemporary described as "that fatall Friday morning" in March 1622.

Search as it did, the archaeological team could find no evidence that Wolstenholme Towne had been rebuilt after the Indian attack. All the buildings yielded evidence of burning—including those inside the fort. Had the Indians elsewhere shown a fierce tenacity in their drive to dislodge the English, one might conclude that the Wolstenholme fort was overrun. But they had not. On the contrary, the records show that when faced with even token resistance the Indians failed to press their attacks. It is more likely, therefore, that the fort served its purpose and helped save the lives of the settlers who survived, and that later, after the colonists had temporarily vacated it, the Indians returned to loot and set fire to whatever would burn.

Although houses were easily destroyed, palisades were much more fire-resistant and the Indians were unlikely to have taken the trouble to dismantle the defenses. Indeed, the fun of a day's pillaging would have been seriously marred by the hard work of pulling down palisades. In all probability, therefore, the wooden walls, both of the fort and around the "Company Compound," survived for several more years during which time the ponds in both served to water cattle penned inside them.

The core settlement at Wolstenholme Towne appeared to parallel the plans of several contemporary plantation villages in Ulster, comprising only two rows of dwellings and other structures flanking a wide avenue or village green having at one end the "bawne" or fort. That interpretation is of necessity based on very incomplete evidence, for as previously noted, something like half the site may have been eaten away by the eroding river. It would be consistent with other Irish village plans of the same

FIGURE 43.

A male skeleton found in the "Company Compound" appeared to have been buried in haste and to have been a victim of foul play. Dated to the early seventeenth century on the evidence of tobacco pipes found above the bones (top), the man had been swung into the grave by people holding his feet and shoulders (right). A gash above his right eye (below) may have been caused by a blow from a spade.

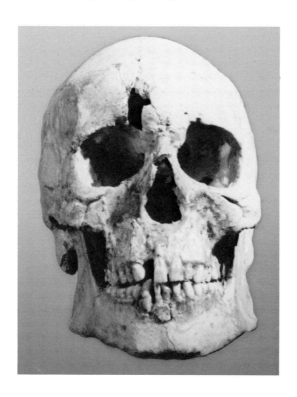

53

period for Wolstenholme Towne's single line to turn east and west when it reached the river, creating a T-shaped configuration. If that were so, the settlement could have been much larger than the surviving remains suggest. However, the equally incomplete historical evidence does nothing to discourage the conclusion that even at the best of times the number of residents was small.

Although 1,500 acres had been set aside for "public land" whereon, presumably, Wolstenholme Towne was located, a remarkable number of apparently independent dwellings and farms have been found within a 500-acre arc around it. Why, then, one must ask were these private properties established on land that should have been public? The only reasonable explanation must be that the 1,500 acres were not contiguous (they were in any case an afterthought) and that when the Martin's Hundred settlements were first established, the farmers thought it safest to build within fleeing distance to the fort. As no shareholder in the Martin's Hundred Society had been assigned less than a hundred acres, it is possible—even likely—that at the outset their tenants' acreage was not in single parcels and that they were content to clear a home farm of perhaps five acres, intending to develop the rest elsewhere in the Society's 21,500 acres as need, labor, and the temper of the times dictated.

That interpretation could explain why several of the excavated sites seem to have been abandoned in the mid-seventeenth century, their owners having moved their homes to the larger and by then equally safe tracts further afield. Many of the early settlers did not live to benefit from the more secure and tranquil years ahead. Such was the case at Site H, a palisaded area barely five hundred feet downriver from the Wolstenholme settlement whose demise was graphically recorded in the ground. Its close proximity to the company village, coupled with the discovery there of three more Augsburg seals identical to those from the "Potter's Pond," led the archaeologists to call it a suburb of Wolstenholme Towne.

Like buildings in the main settlement, those within the Site H palisades had burned; although defined by a convincing number of post-holes, their testimony was not nearly as clear as it had

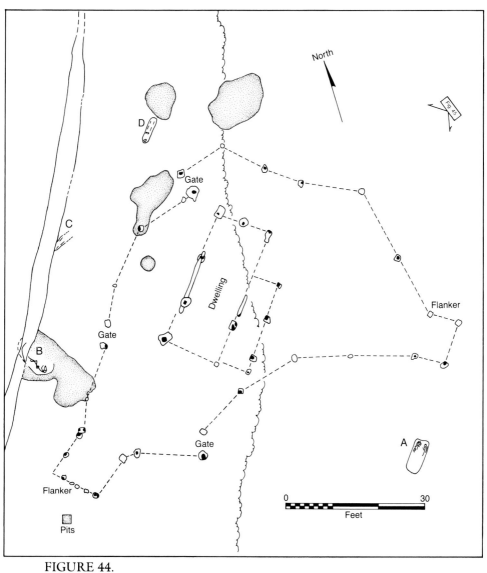

FIGURE 44.

A simplified plan of Site H showing the post-hole patterns for a dwelling and the palisade surrounding it. Human remains were found at "A" (the multiple burial), "B" ("Granny"), "C" (the "Key Lady"), and "D" (another woman).

55

been at other sites. Furthermore, there is doubt as to whether the Site H palisade protected a single large dwelling or a relatively small house having one or more dependencies. Figure 44 simplifies the picture by including only those holes that support the "big house" interpretation, but the photograph *(Figure 45)* shows that on the ground the problem was more complex.

Superficially easier to interpret were the occupants of several holes outside the impaled enclosure. Three of them contained

FIGURE 45.
Site H in course of excavation, the four holes for its southeast flanker in the left foreground (see Figure 44).

the skeletons of women, and another the badly decayed bones of four people buried head to toe. Of these last, the sex of only one could be determined. The remains of a countryman's shoe still covered the right foot, about the pelvis stretched the stain of a decayed leather belt, and close by lay two musket balls, apparently once carried in a pouch attached to it. These, and not the barely discernible traces of the bones, identified this member of the quartet as male. All four died at the same time and presumably of the same causes, but unlike the man in the "Company Compound" the bones were too decayed to tell whether the people had been felled by Indians or by disease.

Like the man with his musket balls, the sex of one of the three separately buried women was revealed not by her bones but by her possessions. Only her legs survived, but between them lay a small iron key, and against the outside of the right femur, a brass thimble. The key had almost certainly hung from a cord around her waist as had a small bag (then called a pocket) in which the woman had kept her thimble.

Best preserved of all the Site H skeletons was that of another of the three women. She lay, not in a grave, but against the side of a partially filled rubbish pit, and in a position of repose, her legs slightly flexed and her right hand up to her head (*Figure 46*). Around her skull rested the roughly bent remains of a once springy iron band intended to secure a linen cap or a fabric-covered roll over which she had dressed her hair. No other traces of clothing could be found, although small clothing hooks, pins, and an iron buckle were discovered elsewhere in the pit.

Known to the archaeologists as "Granny" because she had lost her lower molars, the woman was only about forty years old when she died. Trying to discover *how* she died and who she was provided a classic example of the reliance that archaeologists must place on scholars in other disciplines. Physical anthropologists, pathologists from the office of the Virginia State Medical Examiner, a doctor specializing in sleep patterns, cultural historians, a clothing specialist from London, and a button expert from Holland all helped in interpreting how "Granny" met her death in a rubbish pit.

FIGURE 46.
The skeleton of a woman found in a rubbish pit at Site H and affectionately named "Granny" by the archaeologists.

When first found, the band around the woman's head suggested that she was a person of prominence, but subsequent historical research coupled with the realization that the band had been repaired has led to the conclusion that "Granny" was a servant in the household of John and Sara Boys. He was warden of Martin's Hundred and the senior resident official prior to the arrival of Governor Harwood in 1620. Reconstruction work at Site H demonstrated that the palisade's southwest flanker was large enough to take a cannon of saker size and that mounted there it would have commanded the river far better than it could from the Wolstenholme fort. Located beside a spring-fed ravine running down to the river, the Site H palisade dominated both the fresh water supply and access to the main settlement.

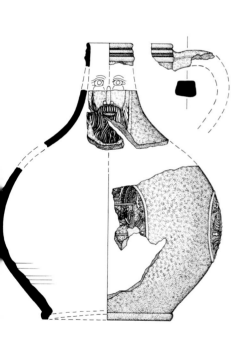

FIGURE 47.

A Rhenish stoneware bottle from Site H (left) was one of two from the site decorated with variations on the arms of the German duchies of Julich, Cleve, Ravensburg, and Mark. Those arms also adorn the intact example (right) recovered from a ship wrecked in the South Atlantic in 1613.

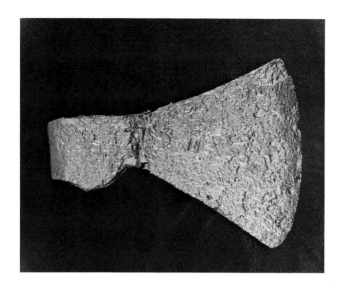

FIGURE 48.

An iron ax stamped with the P.P. initials of its maker. Found at Site H, and broken at the junction of blade and socket, the two parts were discovered in pits sixty feet from each other.

It is reasonable to deduce that Warden Boys built his own fortified house on Martin's Hundred's assigned acres while most of the *Gift of God*'s settlers were still housed near Jamestown. Thus, Site H was in effect the first fort, though it later assumed the status of a suburb and an artillery outwork. The list of dead in the 1622 Indian attack on the Boys homestead included four male servants (presumably those in the multiple grave) and "A Maide" who is believed to be "Granny." Left for dead, she escaped to hide in a trash pit, only to die from loss of blood.

Reports of "Granny's" tragic death fired the popular imagination, and like those of the male "massacre victim" from Wolstenholme Towne itself, they tended to upstage the site's broader cultural importance. More armor and gun parts were recovered, some of the items as yet unparalleled in American and British museum collections. The wealth of potsherds included fragments of Rhenish stoneware Bellarmine bottles, one of whose medallions could be closely paralleled by an intact example subsequently purchased in England *(Figure 47)*. The latter had come from another archaeological site—the wreck of the *White Lion,* a Dutch ship lost in the Atlantic near St. Helena in 1613—its cargo thus helping to date the Site H bottle prior to the 1622 uprising.

Although most people assume that artifacts are the warp and weft of archaeology, they are in reality no more than clues to mysteries older than those faced by criminologists yet otherwise remarkably similar. Inanimate objects are the evidence of who did what and to whom, and interpreting their meaning and putting them in the right order leads, or should lead, to a solution. The principal difference between archaeological and police detection, however, is that archaeologists have no witnesses to question and no criminal to confess and prove them right. Consequently, the list of the unsolved mysteries is longer than the solved. Thus, for example, an ax found at Site H has an intriguing story to tell. The blade was recovered from a rubbish pit outside the north palisade, but the socket or poll was found sixty feet away in the filling of "Granny's" pit *(Figure 48)*. How did the ax break and why were the pieces deposited so far from each other?

Those questions and others like them have never been answered. Nevertheless, four years of digging in Martin's Hundred have provided a wealth of information about life and death in the dangerous, weaning years of the Virginia colony. That the Indians—and our latter-day taste for sensationalism—have placed the emphasis on death and destruction rather than on endurance and growth is understandable but no less regrettable. In truth, the dramatically short-lived failure at Wolstenholme Towne was not an end but a beginning. Survivors returned; new families came over to replace those who had been killed. Slowly, and in the face of later and even more devastating adversities, the people of Martin's Hundred put down roots from which good things grew.

Just as swords can be hammered into plowshares, so the site of the fort at Wolstenholme became an orchard. More than a century and a half would pass before the wagons of war disturbed the peace of the acres that by then were known as Carter's Grove. The great eighteenth-century house that still dominates the landscape and the people who lived in it did not materialize, new-born and fresh-faced, out of virgin ground. They were the products of a history that stretched back through many generations to a day in 1619 when, off the bow of the *Gift of God*, a thin gray line on the horizon parted ocean and sky and a seaman cried "Land ho!"—or perhaps "Your eyesight's better than mine. Doesn't that look like . . .?"

ILLUSTRATION SOURCES

FIGURE 2.   Detail from a map of Virginia drawn by John Farrer and published in London in 1651. Courtesy, William M. Clements Library, University of Michigan, Ann Arbor.

FIGURE 8.   Photograph by Victor Boswell. Courtesy, National Geographic Society.

FIGURE 10.   Sir Henry Paiton by Daniel Mytens, 1621. Courtesy, collection of Sir Hereward Wake, Bt.

FIGURE 13.   Detail from Jan Steen's *The Poultry Yard,* 1660. Courtesy, Mauritshuis, The Hague.

FIGURE 18.   Prince Charles Stuart by Sir Anthony van Dyck, 1641. Courtesy, collection of Sir Hereward Wake, Bt.

FIGURE 21.   Painting by Richard Schlecht. Courtesy, National Geographic Society.

All other illustrations are the property of the Colonial Williamsburg Foundation, as are the excavated and antique objects.

Number*	Colonial Williamsburg Catalog Number	Measurements
7	7171. C.G. 1737A	Length 21¼″
8	7172. C.G. 1773B 7173. C.G. 1773B 7174. C.G. 1760D	Length of date $9/16$″
9	7175. C.G. 1737L	Diam. 3¾″
10	7176. C.G. 1771D 7177. C.G. 1773D	Length 1⅜″
11	7178. C.G. 1771E	Height 11⁵/₁₆″
12	7179. C.G. 1776B	Height 7¹³/₁₆″
13	C.W. 1982-83	Height 6½″
14	7180. C.G. 1760A	Height 4¹⁵/₁₆″
15	7181. C.G. 1773E	Height 13³/₁₆″
16	7182. C.G. 2115B	Est. Height 13⁹/₁₆″
17	7183. C.G. 2115E	Rim Diam. 10⅞″
18	7184. C.G. 2115A	Width 7³/₁₆″
19	C.W. 1978-16	Length 21¾″
20	C.W. G-1977-308 7185. C.G. 2076B 7186. C.G. 2115A	Length 39″ Link Diam. ½″ Link Diam. 7/₁₆″
22	7187. C.G. 3050E	Height 13½″
27	No Number	Height 26⅜″
28	7188. C.G. 3050F 7189. C.G. 1737L	Rim Diam. 2⁵/₁₆″ Base Diam. 2⅝″
31	7190. C.G. 3113A 7191. C.G. 4085B 7192. C.G. 3113C	Diam. ¾″ Diam. ¾″ Diam. ¹³/₁₆″
32	7193. C.G. 3113F	Length 18⅝″

*All numbering of multiple item illustrations is from left to right and from top to bottom.

Number	Colonial Williamsburg Catalog Number	Measurements
33	7194. C.G. 3113F	Diam. 13″
	7195. C.G. 3113F	Diam. 11³⁄₈″
	7196. C.G. 3113F	Height 3³⁄₄″
	7197. C.G. 3113F	Height 4³⁄₄″
	7198. C.G. 3113F	Height 7¹³⁄₁₆″
34	7199. C.G. 3113F	Diam. 12⁵⁄₈″
35	7200. C.G. 3113F	Height 3³⁄₄″
36	7201. C.G. 3113F	Length 13¹⁄₄″
37	7202. C.G. 3113F	Surviving Length 28¹⁄₈″ Average Shot Gauge .1328″
38	7203. C.G. 3113F	Height 11″
39	7204. C.G. 3011H	Length 6¹³⁄₁₆″
	7205. C.G. 3375C	Length 1⁵⁄₁₆″
	7202. C.G. 3113F	Length 28¹⁄₈″
	7206. C.G. 3016C	Length 15¹³⁄₁₆″
	C.W. 1978-9	Length 59″
	7207. C.G. 3016A	Length ³⁄₁₆″
40	C.W. 1977-415	Hilt Height 6¹⁄₂″
	7208. C.G. 1821A	Pommel Diam. 1⁵⁄₈″
	7209. C.G. 2105C	Height 5″
41	C.W. 1978-20	Length 15¹⁄₄″
	7210. C.G. 3016E	Length 12¹⁄₂″
42	C.W. 1978-21	Length 13″
	7211. C.G. 3113F	Length 5³⁄₁₆″
43	C.G. 3092G	Est. Stature 5′9″
47	7212. C.G. 4115D	Height 9⁵⁄₈″
	C.W. 1982-84	Height 7⁵⁄₈″
48	7213. C.G. 4143A	Socket Length 3″
	7213a. C.G. 4115A	Blade Length 5⁹⁄₁₆″